"Short Cuts" and American Life and Society in early Nineties

By Hasti Sardashti

authorHOUSE®

AuthorHouse™ UK Ltd.
500 Avebury Boulevard
Central Milton Keynes, MK9 2BE
www.authorhouse.co.uk
Phone: 08001974150

First published by AuthorHouse 10/25/2011

ISBN: 978-1-4567-9612-9 (sc)

*To all the books and movies that took me
through my childhood and after*

Acknowledgments

I want to thank Jessica Zoya Sardashti for her editorial help and for encouraging me to be less fragmented and more linear, and to be more expressive and not to hide. I also want to thank all my friends and family that all through the years encouraged me for my passion for films and in particular for Robert Altman's 'Short Cuts'. My special thanks go to the University of Nottingham. If I hadn't received those regular phone calls from them to check on me and encourage me to pursue my passion for films, I might have never got this far.

Contents

Introduction

> "Part of the miracle of Robert Altman's triumphantly fierce, funny, moving and innovative Short Cuts is that you can't get this movie out of your head. You keep playing it back to savor its formula-smashing audacity. Its peerless performances and its cleareyed view of blasted lives."
>
> Rolling Stone/ Peter Travers

I was in Germany when I went to see Short Cuts at my local independent cinema in 1993. I don't remember why I went, but I remember that I came out feeling very impressed, that it was a great film and that the director (Altman) was a genius. I was impressed by the stories and how the film was made, all these characters in nine different households, connecting and interacting. I had never seen something like that before. It was a time of transition in my life. Germany and the whole world were also going through a big transition. It was just few years after the fall of the Berlin Wall (Die Mauer), which led to West and East Germany's reunification. The end of the Cold War, was just too confusing and scary for me. I grew up during the Cold War era in a neighboring country of Soviet Union, and in a family where socialism and sense of justice and respect for the working class was not a belief but a religion. Like many others from developing countries, I grew up with the genuine belief that only with the support of Soviet Union we can become free and reach political and economical independence from the west. So all that happening in the early 1990's gave me a terrible sense of shock, fear, helplessness and grief. Having experienced pre and post revolution in Iran during my teenage years, my world seemed to have turned upside down again in the early 90's when I was just turning thirty.

In 1993 I was in my last year of qualifying as a medical doctor. I never thought that ten years later I would be living in England, feeling frustrated with my medical training and undertaking masters in film studies. It seems if all through these years Robert Altman's Short Cuts continued to stay on my mind, and when I had to choose my final dissertation in 2004 I only could think of one film: Short Cuts. Although I made several discoveries through my work that could explain my fascination with Short Cuts, I still didn't feel that I had completely understood my connection to Short Cuts, and I still couldn't get the movie out of my mind. A year later I happened to join a social gathering of some Irish psychiatrists in London, one of them a good friend of mine, who introduced me to the group as the one who studied film. The group showed interest in my work. They encouraged me to send a copy of my writing to Mr Altman. They even drafted a letter for me starting with "Dear Mr Altman I admire your work...". Few months later I sent a copy of my work to Mr Altman, believing it would never arrive, and would be never be read by anyone especially not by Mr Altman. I could not believe my eyes when few months later, in the beginning of 2006, I received an e-mail from Mr Altman's PA saying Mr Altman 'is honored by my hard work and that he wishes me the best of luck'.

I was extremely saddened (and still am) by Robert Altman's sudden death in November 2006. My life happened to take different turns since and I went through several other transitions in my life.

I believe my desire to publish my thoughts about Short Cuts in recent years, came out my deep appreciation for a great director and artist, to whom I am connected. That is also an act of not wanting to be afraid of following my curiosity and intuitions by going over my boundaries and doing what I feel doing even if not knowing why.

In following chapters I will discuss first my thoughts on the content of Short Cuts as a representation of American life and society in the early Nineties. I will then focus on the film itself and its structure and discuss some thoughts on classical and post classical Hollywood cinema as well as Robert Altman's cinema.

Short Cuts: a representation of the American society and American life in the early Nineties

The role of Television news and the political, social and economical changes in 1990's America

Just in the first few minutes of Short Cuts' opening sequence the most frightening issues the Americans were facing in the early Nineties are presented to the audience in an intelligent and symbolic way. The political changes and transitions in the world and the subsequent fears the Americans were facing that time: the fear of war , terrorism, or the treat of natural disasters with a subsequent sense of helplessness and hopelessness.

A few minutes into of Short Cuts' opening sequence, we hear and see Howard Finnigan's Editorial, discussing the war on the Medflies (00:02:08): "Time is come to go to war again, not with Iraq, not international terrorists, or what was once Yugoslavia, but with medflies"...a potentially devastating insect, what... California makes its new home, despite the spraying...How significant is for the health of public... public is not convinced ... people sense that ...is that a war one can be won? I would say no..."

Donovan and Scherer in their book, Unsilent Revolution: television News and American Public Life, 1948-1991 studied how television news since the 1950s has affected American moods, American society and institutions, and American politics and politicians.[1] During 1989 through 1991 the television coverage of a few dramatic and important events: shootings at Tiananman Square in Beijing, the fall of the Berlin Wall, the Persian Gulf War, and the failed Russian coup affected millions of American television viewers. The effect of television coverage of the final campaign against Iraqi president Saddam Hussein in 1991 was said to have: "restored America's faith in its own role and power in the world, a faith badly shaken in Vietnam."[2]

After watching television coverage of the Vietnam War President Eisenhower said that "it would be impossible for Americans to fight another world war because of television."[3]During the Iraq war, Pentagon made sure that the media coverage of the war remains restricted to facts; television showed troops preparing, artillery pieces firing at unseen targets or fighter planes dropping bombs on factories and bridges. However television didn't show live action or Iraqi corpses. Donovan and Scherer describe how "president Bush successfully exploited the power of television to assure the American people that he had not taken them into futile, open-ended war like the detested

---

1   Donovan, J. Robert. And Scherer, Ray. Unsilent Revolution: television News and American Public Life, 1948-1991. Woodrow Wilson International and Cambridge University Press, USA, 1992, p ix.
2   Ibid. p 308-309.
3   Ibid. p 311.

conflict in Vietnam". [4] Donovan and Scherer point out that President Bush had already good experience of using television as a media for manipulating the public during his 1988 presidential campaign: "television news not only shaped the campaign but also in many fundamental ways was the campaign."[5]

Short Cuts was shot in summer of 1992 in a southern Californian suburbia. It was one year after Operation Desert Storm defeated Iraq and liberated Kuwait. One year after the dissolution of the Soviet Union and the establishment of the Commonwealth of the Independent States (CIS) and one year after declaration of independence from Yugoslavia by Slovenia and Croatia. And it was one year after the outbreak of the Crown Heights Riot, a three-day riot that occurred in August 1991 in the Crown Heights neighborhood in the New York City borough of Brooklyn. Crown Heights was and remains a West Indian and African American community with a large minority of Jews. The riots began after the child of two Guyanese immigrants was accidentally killed by an automobile in the motorcade of a prominent Hasidic rabbi. The riot unveiled the long tension between the Crown Heights' black and Jewish communities and had an impact on the 1993 mayoral race, which on the end led to improving the relationships between the two communities. Short Cuts was shot during George Senior Bush's presidency, and Bill Clinton's campaign for presidential election and few months after the south central riots in Los Angeles, where 54 people were killed, 2,383 were known to have been injured, and 13,212 people were arrested. There was an estimated $700 million in property damage in Los Angeles County.

---

4   Ibid. p 313.
5   Ibid. pp 240-257.

Television news made America once more the focus of national and international attention in 4 March, 1991, when KTLA-TV channel 5, broadcasted a 81 second report about the assault on Rodney King, an African American, by L.A. police officers. On 3 March, 1991 Rodney King was driving a car in L.A. when he was signaled by a police car behind him. Rodney ignored the signal and when police finally stopped the car, Rodney was treated by the police with 56 baton blows and six kicks, in a period of two minutes, producing 11 skull fractures, brain damage, and kidney damage. A man named George Holliday, standing on the balcony of a nearby building, videotaped the incident, and gave his tape to channel 5 on the following day. Unaware of the tape, the police officers involved in the incident (all white Americans) filed inaccurate reports about the injuries they inflicted on Rodney. On 15 March, 1991, four police officers were charged with assault of Rodney and on 26 March they pleaded not guilty. The trial of these officers was relocated from L.A. to the suburb of Simi Valley, in Ventura County. The jury was selected from a neighborhood with a white American population in which many people have friends or family members who were police officers. After a year the trial started on 5 March, 1992, and on 29 April, 1992, the jury acquitted the four defendants. Thousands of people in South Central L.A. responded to the verdict by rioting for several days. The violence spread to other parts of Los Angeles County and federal troops and the California National Guard were mobilized. During six days of rioting, 54 people were killed, 2,383 were known to have been injured, 13,212 people were arrested and there was an estimated $700 million in property damage in Los Angeles County.[6]

In his book Popular Film and American Culture (1994), Joseph Natoli compares the rioters to controversial presidential candidate Ross Perot. Perot ran as a candidate of the Reform Party against Republican and Democrats in 1992, with his slogan of "action not words". Natoli describes his understanding of the events as following:

> "They were driven to violent actions by a society incapable of identifying or correcting its own injustices. Our society has moved so far from anything natural, either a natural law or a natural perception of what is dehumanising, that the natural thing to do is to rise up and revolt. Riot and break through by this unsayable action the horrendous lived experience of our calcified society."[7]

Natoli (1994) is not surprised that the revolts and rioters rise up when the political parties in America moved far from seeing and responding to the problems of "this country." "Politics has become nothing more than a devious spinning of powerbrokers and shareholders, lobbyists propel decisions, the media controls representation and therefore controls the realising of our democracy. Conspiracy theories intersect Baudrillard's simulacra, the power of the sign crosses the power of the wealthy. And

---

6   Delk, James D. Fires and Furies: The L.A. Riots – what Really Happened. Etc Pubns, California, 1994.

7   Natoli, Joseph. Hauntings: Popular Film and American Culture 1990-1992. State University of New York Press, Albany, 1994, pp 47-49.

then Perot and the rioters rise up."[8] Natoli suggests that there are different kinds of revolts and different kinds of rising ups: "Perot's revolt is that of the father, the anger of the father, the rioters' revolt is that of the son and daughter, the rebellion of sons and daughters."[9]

During the 1980s the use of Cable TV and VCR in American households exploded. By the end of 1992 ninety eight percent of all American homes had television sets and 78 percent possessed VCR.[10] In Short Cuts, TV sets appear in almost all the households, the public places, and even in limousines. The TV sets run all the time in the background of each scene. For example the TV news is running while Lori Kaisers is on the phone with one of her telephone sex clients and feeds her child at the same time. The role of the television in the Short Cuts is not only restricted to the television news and its affect of the life of Americans, it is also representing the exploitation of the power of the television and its long standing effect on people's perception of the reality and their consequent reaction or lack of reaction.

Altman's vision throughout Short Cuts communicates his belief that the connective tissue in American life between the imaginary and reality is severed."[11] Stuart Kane and his two friends are very ordinary white middle class men on a fishing trip. On their trip they enjoy making the middle aged Doreen Piggot bend down in the 24 hours diner she works just for them to have an other look at her buttocks. Once arrived at their fishing

8   Natoli, Joseph. Hauntings: Popular Film and American Culture 1990-1992. State University of New York Press, Albany, 1994, pp 47-49.

9   Ibid.

10   Ibid. p 341.

11   Kaplan, Mike and Dorr, John. Luck, Trust, and Ketchup: Robert Altman In Carver Country. Videotext, 1993.

spot they discover the naked body of a young girl in the river, but instead of responding responsibly by adequately reporting the incident to the police they decide to leave the body for three days while they fish in the same river. They are not only unresponsive to the naked, dead body of the girl and unsympathetic to this human condition, but also very disrespectful as they urinate in the river over the body and take pictures of her. They appear to be armored against all visuals, all signs of lived experience. Of course they have seen this sort of naked, young woman's dead body in a river before, in the movies or in television.

There are also other scenes where the characters appear unresponsive and emotionally unaffected by the reality. When Howard Finnigan's father played by Jack Lemmon, arrives at the hospital few hours before Finnigan's little boy dies, all he seems to care about is boasting about being the father of a famous television news editor, or later about his confession to his son about his affair with his mother's sister when Howard was little. He is unresponsive and paralyzed when the little boy dies, and leaves the hospital without a word of comfort to his son. In Lori Kaiser's case, she seems unaffected by doing telephone sex at home in front of her children and her husband. She doesn't understand that this might affect her family as at the end of the day, she does not practice any sex with strange men, and it is all in their imagination.

I wonder if dissociating from the reality encouraged by films and television has been found helpful by the Americans as a way to cope with their day to day fears as well as with their greater fears and nightmares such as fear of war, terrorism, or natural disasters as shown in Short Cuts.

Short Cuts: Fear and Helplessness, Locus of Control and beliefs in Luck and Fate

When Altman first spoke to the poet Tess Gallagher, Raymond Carver's widow, about wanting to make Short Cuts, he told her he wasn't going to be pristine in his approach to Carver and that the stories were going to be scrambled. Gallagher instinctively recognised and encouraged his choice, and said Carver admired Nashville, "that he liked the helplessness of those characters and their ability to manage nevertheless." [12]

Altman viewed all Carver's stories as 'one story', for him Carver's stories were all 'occurrences', all about things that 'just happen to people' and 'cause their lives to take a turn'. Tess Gallagher describes how Altman and Carver were drown to the theme of 'luck'; " both of them chancers and creators willing to stake their lives, artistic and otherwise, on the precarious rim of possibility. They've known the dive and swoop of fortune which takes us a step beyond mere courage to that helpless place we all hit at some point where we realise anything could and does happen, and to us." [13] Altman described how Carver's view of the world, is similar to his own and that it "maybe termed dark by some". "We're connected by similar attitudes about the arbitrary nature of luck in the scheme of things such as Finnigan's child being hit by a car in "A Small, Good Thing"; the Kanes' marriage upheaval resulting from a body being discovered during a fishing trip in "So Much Water So Close to Home."[14]

---

12 Carver, Raymond. Short Cuts, "with an Introduction by Robert Altman", The Harvill Press, London, 1993, pp 8-9.
13 Altman, robert and Barhydt, Frank. Short Cuts, The Screenplay. Capra press, Santa Barbara, 1993, p. 9.
14 Carver, Raymond. Short Cuts, "with an Introduction by

In Short Cuts Altman brings his emphasis on the randomness of natural disasters, an earthquake, in order to picture the greater levels of lack of control by the individuals. Clearly any natural disaster affects every one and no one has any actual control over it. We all feel helpless by natural disasters and definitely if we happen to survive the disaster, it is a matter of luck. I believe Altman's choice to use the song "Prisoner of Life" during and particularly at the end of the film while the camera is panning over L.A., is also an attempt of symbolising these feelings of helplessness and lack of control.

Julian B. Rotter's in his social learning theory describes 'locus of control' as a person's perception of the cause of life events. Someone with an internal locus of control would generally perceive one as responsible for certain occurrences, while a person with an external locus of control would most often blame or thank fate, destiny, luck, society or some other environmental force beyond his or her control. Rotter warns that locus of control is neither a typology nor a proposition. Rotter acknowledges that the locus of control does predict people's behaviour in most situations, however, there may be some specific situations where people, who are generally 'external' behave like 'internals'. He explains that this could happen as their learning history has shown that they have control over the outcome of certain situations, although overall they experience little control over what happens to them in general. [15]

In 1981, Mahler, Greenberg, and Hayashi examined in a study the relationship between different cultures and their beliefs in a 'just world'. They defined the just world

---

Robert Altman", The Harvill Press, London, 1993, pp 8-9.
15   The Social Learning Theory of Julian B. Rotter. http://psych.fullerton.edu/jmearns/rotter.htm.

as a just place where good people are rewarded and bad people are punished. They claim that authoritarianism as a characteristic of western culture, reinforces the notion that the world is just, as do the fairytales and popular myths as well as the western religions. These, as a part of American culture, contribute to a fairly high belief in a just world. Even more influential according to them is the significant finding that Americans tend to have a greater internal locus of control, with a higher sense of control over their life and their environment.[16]

Some twenty years later, in 2001, Beverly Ann Osband explores in her dissertation the phenomena of fate in American society and describes, "when life goes well… as a culture, we (Americans) attribute success to our own hard work, cleverness, intelligence, good timing, luck, and if we have a spiritual orientation, to Divine Providence. When we (Americans) experience reversals, failure, loss, or tragedy,… we question ourselves and our God why, wondering at the unseen forces affecting our lives… In the tension between self-blame and the search for another on whom to place responsibility, the awareness grows of a third, an unseen mover of sorts, which I have come to recognise as fate."[17]

Prior and during the time Altman's Short Cuts was developed and shaped, Americans experienced over a decade of Republican administration, represented by Reagan and Bush extreme right wing national policies and an ill economy. On 9 November 1989 with the fall of the

---

16 Carmona,Liz. Cultural Influence on Just World Beliefs. In Psy 324: Advanced Social Psychology, Spring, 1998, http://www.muohio.edu/psybersite/justworld/culture.shtml.

17 Osband, Beverly Ann. Fate, Suffering, and transformation. In Section B: the Sciencees & Engineering. Vol 61 (9-B), Apr 2001, 5000, US: Univ Microfilms International.

Berlin Wall, America and whole world experienced one of the most extreme changes in the history of the twentieth century: the end of the Cold War and the beginning of a new post-Cold War era. Hardly anyone could have foreseen the end of communism in Russia and in Eastern Europe during that time. The demise of the Soviet Union left the United States the sole remaining superpower, a position that carried its own risks and problems. With this extreme change of dichotomy between the two world powers, on which was the base of the national and international politics for more than fifty years and also a major coping mechanism for the people by splitting between the Good and Bad, God and Evil, Communism and Democracy, in late 1980s and early 1990s it came to a break down of the known structures which were experienced as very frightening by American people.

Altman's critical view and mistrust on politician is well portrayed in his 1975 film, Nashville. Short Cuts is frequently compared by the public and critics with Nashville. Quart and Auster (2002) describe Nashville as a work built on 'observation' rather than exposition, 'intuition' rather than analysis, a vision of a society based on 'chance' rather than on one whose values can be systematically traced to a set of causes... "when Altman's suggestive metaphors and images come alive, as they do in Nashville, they conjure up a monstrous and irrational America which is vivid, resonant, and true."[18]

Altman describes Nashville as the proper place for him to equate the analogy of elected officials and politicians, which in many ways is a popularity contest similar to the success of country and western music."...I wanted to

---

18 Quart.Leonard and Auster. Albert. American Film and Society since 1945. Praeger, Westport, Connecticut, London, 2002, p 107.

do Nashville to study our myths and our heroes and our hypocrisy. Because by the time we usually get around to studying our present, it's past, and the truth is buried so deep we can't even find it."[19]

Nashville comments ironically on some important issues in American society in mid 1970's such as the forced resignation of President Nixon by the Supreme Court due to evidence of his complicity in Watergate scandal.

Cathrine Russel interprets Altman's tragic response to the failure of the "myth" of the presidency in America at the end of Nashville, as a way of describing the role of political assassination in America since Kennedy and Oswald in 1963 as a reciprocal form of violence, which is also "contagious" and spreads throughout the community.[20]

Altman's vision disagrees with Russel's interpretation of Nashville and emphasizes on the randomness of occurrences in the society and people's life: "they are more about what you don't know rather than what you do know...they keep asking me why that happened to that character...why the assassin did what he did on the end of Nashville...I don't know why...if we knew any of that we probably could prevent it..."[21]

---

19   Kass,.m.Judith. Robert Altman: American Innovator. Popular Library, New York, 1978, pp 193-213.
20   Russel, Cathrine. Narrative Mortality: Death, Closure, and New Wave Cinemas. University of Minnesota Press, Minneapolis, London, 1995, p 195.
21   Kaplan, Mike and Dorr. John. Luck, Trust, and Ketchup: Robert Altman In Carver Country. Videotext, 1993.

Short Cuts: American cinema and American family values in the early Ninteis

Short Cuts was shot just one year after Oliver Stone's JFK in 1991. JFK became embroiled in controversy even before it was finished, after the national security correspondent George Ladner from The Washington Post attacked the film and accused Stone of taking liberties with historical facts, including that President Lyndon B. Johnson was a part of a coup d'état to kill Kennedy.

During the 1990s the film industry provided a major source of funds for Clinton's presidential race, and for the Democratic Party. On 16th September 1992 Barbara Streisand headlined a $1.5 million Beverly Hills fundraiser in for Bill Clinton, which was broadcasted on televisions in major American cities. On 3rd November 1992 Bill Clinton was elected as president of United States and on 19 January 1993, Barbara Streisand appears as the closing act in Clinton's inaugural gala.

The films of the pre Clinton era (1980-1992) are dubbed "Reaganite" entertainment. "Reaganite" relates to the social, political, and cultural issues of the Reagan/Bush and Bush/Quayle administration. They also relate to the "reassurance, optimism and nostalgia, qualities embodied in the political persona of Ronald Reagan."[22]

President Reagan encouraged the nation to restore traditional American values in an attempt to revive the "lost American confidence" after the nations' experience of national traumas in 1970s such as Watergate and the Vietnam war.

The nostalgia of Reaganite cinema brought the magic

---

22 Belton, John. American Cinema/American Culture. McGraw-Hill, New York, 1994, p 322.

of the movies back to audiences. The movies of this era took the audience back in the time and gave them the hope of reviving "the small-town affluent American paradise of the Eisenhower era, before poverty, crime, homelessness, and the demise of both the family and community began to erode the American dream."[23] As an example in 1989's Field of Dreams, the main character played by Kevin Costner, seems to present the desire of reviving the nostalgic values of American society when he innocently responds to a mysterious voice that tells him to build a baseball field, American's national pastime, in middle of nowhere, "if you build, he will come", and 'they' came to play on his field, famous, dead baseball players from the past decades, including Joe Jackson.[24]

Costner's character represents innocence as a rejection of urban life and promotion of life in the suburbs or closer to nature. There are several other films from this era like Out of Africa, 1989; Crocodile Dundee, 1986; Gorillas in the Mist, 1988; Dances with Wolves, 1990; City Slickers, 1991, that promote a return to nature, in order to feel content and receive vitality in one's life. "Reaganite" films also encourage a return to conservative values of masculinity by promoting action super-heroes like Rocky and Rambo series as well as Terminator or Die Hard films. Terrorism and drug trafficking, the issues of high importance identified by Reagan administration as the chief threats to the security of 1980s America, are frequently represented in the films of this era. Reaganite films promote law and order, and celebrate the importance of conservative role of the family in order to gain control and feel safe. Next to this a perfectly functioning American economic system and a glamorized

---

23 Ibid. p 325.
24 Ibid.

military system are the other important presentations of American society in Reaganite cinema. Robin Wood describes the dominant tendency of the Reaganite era as "the restoration of patriarchal authority...and with an attempted reconstitution of the nuclear family". [25] During the Reagan-Bush period, for the first time in American history, there were more Americans living in the suburbs than in the cities. John Belton describe this as a move to mark "a return of the American society to small-town values". [26]

In contrast to Reagan and Bush's glorification of traditional family values, Altman portrays emptiness, alcoholism, voyeurism, sexual deviations, emotional dependencies, infidelity, and a lot of unexpressed anger and frustration expressed in some rageous and senseless murder or suicide in these people's lives. Altman liked Carver's stories straight away and felt inspired by his stories to the extend of turning them into a film. Altman believed that "Carver writes about 'inside,...not 'outside', and to Altman 'inside' meant the 'truth'. With Short Cuts Altman said he wanted to show the people, the 'reality', the 'truth' of the American life. When Altman was asked in the documentary 'Making of Short Cuts', what Short Cuts is about, he said that he has to think about a common dominator and the common dominator for Short Cuts would be 'Ketchup' because it is what you find everywhere in American life and American households, it is like a little "alcoholism", a little "infidelity", a little "self-doubt."

President Reagan first acknowledged the issues with AIDS in American society with a belated speech in the mid 1980s, after over 20,000 American had already

---

25   Ibid. p 331.
26   Ibid. p 326.

died from the illness. Reagan blamed the death of these American people on the lack of 'family values'. In a similar way the Vice President Dan Quayle blamed the failure of the economy in 1992, on fictional African-American single mother character, Murphy Brown and a lack of "family values."[27]

In the 1991–1992 season, Murphy Brown became pregnant and as her baby's father was unwilling to give up his own lifestyle to be a parent, Murphy chose to have the child and raise it alone. This story line made the show a subject of political controversy during the 1992 American presidential campaign. On May 19, 1992, in a speech at the Commonwealth Club in San Francisco Dan Quayle criticised the Murphy Brown character for ignoring the importance of fathers by birthing a child alone.

Short Cuts was shot just few months before Bill Clinton became the President of America on 3 November 1992. After Clinton announced in October 1991, that he was a candidate for the presidency, his campaign was nearly sunk by charges of marital infidelity. Clinton's political image survived the charges. In some way Clinton's background story and his private life during his presidency, could represent him as one of the characters in Altman's Short Cuts or Raymond Carver's stories.

William Jefferson Clinton was born on August 1946, in Hope, a small town in Arkansas, just three months after his father an automobile-parts salesman was killed in a car accident. His mother Virginia Cassidy, married Roger Clinton, a car dealer, when Bill was seven. The family moved to Hot Springs, Arkansas where the bright and ambitious Bill attended the public school. Roger Clinton's problems with alcohol and violence, led to a divorce, but the couple remarried soon after. When Bill was 15 as a

---

27 Ibid.

gesture he had his last name legally changed to Clinton. In the summer of 1963, during a trip to Washington D.C., when Bill was a delegate in the American Legion Boys State, he met President John F. Kennedy. Clinton attended Georgetown University, Oxford University as a Rhodes Scholar, and Yale Law School, where he met Hillary Rodham, a fellow law student and political companion. Bill and Hillary married in 1975 a year before he was elected as Arkansas attorney general. In 1978 Bill became the governor of Arkansas. Two years later he was defeated by Republicans, but in 1982 he returned, and remained the governor of Arkansas till he became the president of the United States.

In contrast to Dan Quayle and his official criticism of fictional American sitcom character, Murphy Brown's decision to have a baby out of wedlock in May 1992, emphasising the traditional 'family values' over political and presidential elections, Clinton initiated a strategy of reforms for healthcare, education, and welfare, and pledged to repeal the ban on gay Americans in the military.[28]

In a speech at Wellesley College on 29 May, 1992, Hillary Rodham Clinton publicly challenged Dan Quayle's 'family values':

"If you don't get married, you're abnormal. If you get married but don't have children, you're a selfish yuppie. If you get married and have children but then go outside the home to work you are a bad mother. If you get married and have children but stay home, you've wasted your education. And if you don't get married but have children

---

28 Smith, R. Carol. "Gender and family values in the Clinton presidency and 1990s Hollywood film". In Philip Davis and Paul Wells (Eds.) American film and politics from Reagan to Bush Jr. Manchester University Press, Manchester and New York, 2002, pp 76-88.

and work outside the home as a fictional newscaster, you get in trouble with the Vice President."[29]

Bill Clinton won the presidential election in November 1993 with six millions votes and 172 electoral votes over Bush. The luck seemed to follow Clinton even in the second term of his presidency in 1999 when he was acquitted of accusations and impeachment due to his marital infidelity, when fewer than half the Senators voted to evict him from the presidency.

Hilary Rodham Clinton maybe was a 'bad' mother according to the ideals of Reagan and Bush senior's administration, as she was married, had a child but worked outside the house, but she definitely acted as a 'good' wife. Like Sherri Shepard in Short Cuts, Hillary turned a blind eye to her husband's infidelity and kept the father present, who knows, maybe just in an attempt to avoid another generation of rebellious rioters as it was prophesied by Dan Quayle.

---

29   King, Norman. The Woman in the White House. Birch Lane Press, New York,1996, p 6.

Making of *Short Cuts*

Short Cuts: Pre-Production

> Abraham Polonsky once said: "Adapting
> a book to a film is fundamentally a moral
> crisis,…as the book is not chosen to be
> translated for non-readers."[30]

Robert Altman always liked to read short stories, hoping
to find some material for his films, but he never read
before Raymond Carver, the American short story
writer and poet. Altman encountered Carver first on his
flight back from Italy in 1990 when he opened a book of
Carver's short stories and was felt straightaway "in tune"
with Carver and his stories about contemporary working
class American life. Altman felt that Carver writes "about
inside, not outside", and felt adamant to turn Carver's
stories to a film.

Raymond Carver was called the best American short-
story writer since Hemingway and a hero of perception.
Carver was born in 1938 in Clatskanie, a mill town on

---

30 Kolker, Robert Philip. A Cinema of Loneliness. Third
Edition, Oxford University Press, New York, 2000, p 398.

the Columbia River in Oregon. His father, a sawmill worker, was an alcoholic and died at the age of fifty-three. His mother a victim of domestic violence, worked either as a waitress or as a retail clerk. Carver grew up in Yokima, Washington, where the family moved in 1941. After graduating in 1956 he married the sixteen-year old Maryann Burk, his high-school sweetheart and shortly after their first child was born. Carver supported his family with a list of low paid jobs and Maryann worked as a waitress, sales person, administrator and a teacher. Two years later their second child was born. Between fatherhood, his low paid jobs, and his alcohol habit, Carver found some time to write poems and short stories. He stated "I needed to write something I could get some kind of payment from immediately, hence poems and short stories." [31] After he moved his family to Paradise, California, in 1958, Carver enrolled at Chico State College, where he begun an apprenticeship under John Gardner. Gardner gave him a close and line-by-line criticism and taught him a set of values that were not negotiable. One of the values which Carver held until his death was the conviction that great literature is life-connected, life-affirming, and life-changing. According to Gardner in the best fiction, the central character, the hero or heroine, is also the moved character, the one to whom something happens in the story that makes a difference, something that changes the way character looks at himself and hence the world. Gardner was a humanist as was Carver and as was Chekhov. Art is not self-expression, Carver insisted, it is communication. Carver was described as the American Chekhov. In fact Anton Chekhov (1860-1904) remained Carver's life long mentor. For Carver, Chekhov was the

---

31 Stull, L. William. Biographical Essay. http://www.whitman. edu/english/carver/biography.html.

greatest short-story writer who ever lived. In a way they seem to have led parallel lives. Like Chekhov, Carver was of working class parentage, and knew intimately the marginal lives of hardship, from which he gained the inspiration for his stories. Carver once said, 'they are my people,... I could never write down to them.'

In 1960s Carver got several of his poems published. After his father died in 1967 Carver was accepted for a white-collar job as an editor at Science Research Associates (SRA), and moved his family to San Francisco's suburbs. In 1970 Carver published his first book, Will you Please Be Quite, Please?. After his job at SRA was terminated in 1970 Carver was finally able to write full-time. Carver published Neighbours in June 1971. This was a turning point in his writing career. For Carver Neighbours was a highly stylised story. By 1977 Carver was estranged from his wife Maryann and his children, and was hospitalised four times for alcoholism within a period of a year. Carver said that he felt close to death but decided to live and stopped drinking in 1977. Carver calls his life after this stage as 'his second' life or 'the other life – The one without mistakes.'[32]

Carver met Tess Gallagher, a poet, at a writer's conference. He and Tess shared a similar background. They were both from Pacific Northwest, children of an alcoholic father, and survivors of broken marriages. Tess was Carver's soul mate and life partner until his death in 1988.[33] After Carver's death Tess continued to publish a wide range of Carver's poems and short stories. This included Short Cuts (1993) with an introduction by Robert Altman. The film script for Short Cuts, was written by Barhydt and Altman in close collaboration with Tess

32 Ibid.
33 Ibid.

Gallagher. Knowing about Altman's and Barhydt great sense of dry humour and their love for irony, Gallagher felt that it was her duty to make sure that it is understood that Carver felt very close to his characters and that he never raised himself above the plights of his characters and never would laugh at his characters.[34]

When Altman first spoke to Tess Gallagher about wanting to make Short Cuts, he told her that he is not going to be pristine in his approach to Carver's stories and the stories are going to be scrambled. Altman read all of Carver's writings and filtered it through his own process. His Short Cuts is made of little pieces and basic elements of Carver's creations, "new but not new". Some characters like of Tess and Zoe Trainer were invented by Barhydt and Altman to provide musical bridges in the film. The setting was changed from the Pacific Northwest to a suburban setting in Southern California. "We always tried to stay as close as possible to Carver's world,…in directing Short Cuts, "certain things came straight out of my own sensibility, which has its differences, and this is as it should be."[35] Gallagher admired the way the stories were told in the film: "Altman and Barhydt broke the frames on the stories and allowed the characters to affect each other's worlds or not, as if to suggest that we are more 'in this together' and alone than we ever suspected. Gallagher recognised that the mechanism of the script, picking up and dropping stories at intervals is in order to pull the viewer into it's current, then allow them to re-approach what's going on down river."[36] Gallagher acknowledged

---

34 Ibid.
35 Carver, Raymond. Short Cuts, "with an Introduction by Robert Altman", The Harvill Press, London, 1993, p 10.
36 Altman, Robert & Barhydt, Frank. Short Cuts: The Screenplay. Capra Press, Santa Barbara, 1993, pp 8-10.

the differences between Carver stories and Altman's interpretation of the stories in Short Cuts and stated that Carver would have had shown a "generous curiosity about the new shape his stories would inevitably take."[37]

Robert Kolker describes in A Cinema of Loneliness, that "Carver's work would not immediately suggest an Altman's film"...But the two share a dark, even misanthropic, view of human behaviour, and especially of gender relationship. Kolker believes that 'isolation' is a mark of Carver's fiction, and that the individual and couples are meanly or sadly contained within their small fictional world: "...Altman, in Short Cuts, creates an interlocking web of narrative not only by having the characters appear within each other's stories, but through often ironic internal references: parallel physical movements or gestures, television sets showing images that imitate or mock the characters' actions, counterpointing and associating them across the narrative field. He turns the sense of isolation and gender panic that is explicit in his own work and inherent in Carver's into a global statement."[38]

Short Cuts: Production

For Altman the process of making a film is "the only thing of value" to him:

"The afterglow, the after-burn of it is nice and it's memorable, but it doesn't...the process itself is being in the activity itself, while it's happening, and really being

---

37 Kaplan, Mike and Dorr, John. Luck, Trust, and Ketchup: Robert Altman In Carver Country. Videotext, 1993.
38 Kolker, Robert Philip. A Cinema of Loneliness. Third Edition, Oxford University Press, New York, 2000, pp 398.

out of control. It starts with the preparation: the script, the casting, then the shooting process, then editing."[39]

Short Cuts was shot in L.A. during summer of 1992. Its unique cast, incorporated some Hollywood favourites such as, legendary actor Jack Lemmon and several well known artists from the music world; Annie Ross, Lyle Lovett, and Tom Waits.

Altman claims that eighty-five to ninety-five percent of his creative work is completed by the time actors are cast, as the bulk of the creative work is then turned over to those actors that he casts. Altman praises the actors for letting themselves being thrown into a situation they only have creative control of the role and not of the entire project. In Short Cuts Altman said that what he really tried to do with his actors was "to get them to be less creative and just use their own natural selves more, as if they were the character in that circumstance."[40]

Altman gave his cast all nine original stories of Short Cuts and the poem Lemonade. According to Altman "many went to read more of Ray's work." Altman filmed one story each week, therefor only three or four of the actors appeared together at once. The first family filmed was Earl and Doreen Piggot. Altman described their work as 'superb' and the rest that followed went "beyond or sideways from his expectations, as they took over by redefining their roles".[41]

Altman believed that what was shot first affects significantly every other subsequent shots in the film. He believed if he "went back and made another start point, it

39 Breskin, David. Inner Views: Filmmaker in conversation. Faber and Faber, Boston, London, 1992, p 272.
40 Ibid. pp 272-286.
41 Carver, Raymond. Short Cuts, "with an Introduction by Robert Altman", The Harvill Press, London, 1993, p 10.

would be a different film"…and he meant "surprisingly" different…"the weather is never the same, the actors never feel the same, not having the same amount of confidence or fear,…it's back to Einstein and relativity: everything is in movement in relationship to everything else, so nothing is ever the same."[42]

Altman was famous for respecting each member of his team and appreciating everybody's work. He saw himself more as someone who just chose people to work together and collaborate on his projects. "I don't 'direct' people. It's a misnomer. I'm just calling the shots. I'm the one who says: 'We have to start here today, and we end here, and we're going to do this now, or we're not going to shoot that."[43] To me it is just a humble statement of Altman's leadership skills. Just looking at some comments made by most actors who worked with him, there is no doubt that Altman was a good leader and a just and nurturing parental figure. As any good parents Altman remained calm, attentive and clear in his interaction with his actors, and provided them with the potential space to play knowing that this would bring the best out of them. The assistant director of Short Cuts, Allan Nicollos described how Altman created "a comfortable place for everybody to come and play and everybody came and played, and that was what we ended up doing."[44]

Altman knew who he was hiring. He made sure that everybody was comfortable with each other and liked each other, and that a feeling of belonging to a "community" is present. Altman showed his appreciation of every one's

---

42 Breskin, David. Inner Views: Filmmaker in conversation. Faber and Faber, Boston, London, 1992, p 275.

43 Ibid. p 283.

44 Kaplan, Mike and Dorr, John. Luck, Trust, and Ketchup: Robert Altman In Carver Country. Videotext, 1993.

contribution on the set by including their ideas. For example the idea of having a clown character in the film came from Tim Robbins, but it was Altman's idea to make it as Claire's occupation. Altman asked Jennifer Jason Lee to write her dialogues on the phone after doing some research, or included the idea with the fish tank coming from Stephen Altman, production designer.

Jack Lemmon described that the "trust" was the major reason that made working with Altman comfortable. Lemmon believed that as an actor once "you can trust you try your best." according to Lemmon one of the biggest assets of a great director like Altman, is also his kind of 'editorial skill': "Altman let the actors to do their part how they want to and he edits out, not the good parts ..."[45] Walt Lloyd, director of photography of Short Cuts worked with several directors, who used improvisation but with Altman he said it was not like that at all. "I can not tell the difference, you can not tell unless you are behind the camera."[46] Frances McDormand liked working with Altman because of the way Altman structured the storytelling of the scene, "technically is that he shoots master shots, that means that whole play is out and you can play whole scene, he doesn't do a lot of coverage of the scenes, a lot of close ups, inserts, ..., as an actor you have not been asked to do the scene maybe more than six times... and it is also something fresh about it,..., he frequently throws some little titbit in the original blueprint of the script, to bring more spark into it..."[47] With Altman the camera is so truthful says Anne Archer ..."you are never asked to produce something artificial,

---

45 Ibid.
46 Ibid.
47 Ibid.

Altman sees what the actors are doing and he asks the camera to capture it...."[48]

When Bob Altman called Julianne Moore about her role, he told her about the scene where Marian was going to be nude and asked her, how she felt about it..."I was doing nudity in another film by that time and not convinced if really it was necessary... but he had something especial in mind, he had an image, and it was clear to me that it was not a sexual image, and I thought it is great; how often do you see nudity in a non sexual way, you always see nudity in a sexual way, I think sometimes for the women, that is what objectifies them and make it difficult for us to do it, but here the nudity is kind of the part of the peoples' life, if you think, only your husband can see you..."[49] Lori Singer was amazed by the expression of sexuality in Short Cuts, feeling that it supported the humanness of everybody, "it is like real life, a lot of vibration..."[50] Altman believed that sexuality had a big meaning in all of these character's lives and Carver's stories, but in Short Cuts the sexuality is not overt and "it seems to be more undercurrent."[51]

Short Cuts was Madeleine Stow's first experience working with Altman: ..."well, it is fun, because when you are a woman and you are doing sort of more with the mainstream pictures ... they really demand of how you have to behave... I can behave like a fishwife here and do what ever and be shrill, you are allowed here... because it is how the human being is... when we started talking about these scenes, he said just do what you want, and

---

48   Ibid.
49   Ibid.
50   Kaplan, Mike and Dorr, John. Luck, Trust, and Ketchup: Robert Altman In Carver Country. Videotext, 1993.
51   Ibid.

we shoot it…and I thought …it is really interesting, first because I haven't had the guts of doing this and then I thought how he comes to work, …it didn't look like a lot of preparation,… and we sat down at rehearsals and all was very free flowing, and we sat down at work and he exactly knew what is going to happen, even if he says he doesn't know, he can tell us what exactly he wants us to do, …and he comes up to you and asking to add lines if the scene is not working out, and it is the way you can sink with him….what is so unique about the film is that, it is everything about small things, about "behaviour"… it is more surprising and interesting,…you just wish that more films would do this and not so plot driven,…"[52] The three hours long Short Cuts is definitely not plot driven and does not comply with rules and standards of traditional Hollywood story telling. There is no relationship between cause and effect and no linear plot progression.

Robert Kolker describes in A Cinema of loneliness (2000) that"The narrative structure of almost all of Altman's films develops out of, or as part of, their spatial structure […] The movement from centre to periphery demands an abandonment of straightforward narrative development. Events on the edges gain equal importance with events in the middle. More is seen and heard than one is accustomed to […] People and events are always disrupted in an Altman film, as are viewer's expectations and assumptions. […] His films do not merely contain unexpected turns; they are unexpected turns. They are quiet attempts at a deconstruction of the narrative and generic truths that are taken for granted in American film, which Altman unfastens from their position as absolutes and relocates within the formal, cultural, ideological structures that created them. In dislocating

---

52 Ibid.

their visual and narrative centres, the films dislocate their generic centres as well and begin to reveal some of the ways in which the smooth, undistracted, and unquestioning forms of cinematic storytelling have lied. Altman will no more construct alternative truths to the lies he perceives than will any other American filmmaker, but the deconstruction is insightful, funny, sometimes angry, sometimes off the mark, and always respectful of uncertainty and plurality.[53]

In Robert Altman's America, Helene Keyssar points out that Altman's films do not present a conceptual conclusion of the world projected in his films as being complete and distinct from the world in which we live. In Altman's films, the motivation for characters' behaviour remains unknown and "the centre of the film exists elsewhere than in the obvious narrative."[54]

Short Cuts: Structure

"My idea of what a great movie will be some day, will be something the audience will watch and it will be very nonlinear and they will walk away with it not being able to articulate what they think about it. I'm more interested in the subliminal reality. I'm more interested in touching people on an unconscious basis to where they sense something rather than intellectually know or agree to something (Robert Altman, 1992)."[55]

---

53 Kolker. Robert. A Cinema of Loneliness; Penn, Kubrick, Scorsese, Spielberg, Altman. Third edition. Oxford University Press, New York, 200, pp346-347

54 Keyssar, Helene. Robert Altman's America. Oxford University Press, New York, 1991, p 16.

55 Altman, Robert. Scene commentary. The Player. 1992. Videodisc. Santa Monica, Calif.: Voyager, 1992.

Short Cuts, does not comply with rules and standards of traditional Hollywood story telling. There is no relationship between cause and effect and no linear plot progression. There is no particular story to concentrate on and the story is not plot driven. David Bordwell describes the principles of causality and motivation as the classical guidelines for the construction of the film's story by the viewer on the basis of the plot. A film's plot usually transmits story information in classical narration and makes these guidelines applicable.[56]

Hollywood classical narrative is linear, it is goal-driven, and it moves through character-based causality towards a logical conclusion. It's realism and its causality is mainly expressed through the character psychology and its development. Bordwell states that in Hollywood cinema, a specific sort of narrative causality operates as the dominant, making temporal and spatial systems vehicles for it.[57] Bordwell descries the causality as the prime unifying principle; "Analogies between characters, settings, and situations are certainly present, but at the denotative level and any parallelism is subordinated to the movement of cause and effect."[58] When confronted with anomalies of the continuous linear causality of classical narrative, as in the case of melodramatic attributes like spectacle, episodic presentation, or dependence on coincidence, Bordwell describes these anomalies as "generic conventions" operating as limited plays "within

---

56 Bordwell, David. Staiger, Janet and Thompson, Kristin. "Classical narration". The Classical Hollywood Cinema : Film Style and Mode of Production to 1960. Routledge & Kegan Paul, London, Melbourne and Henley, 1985, p24.
57 Ibid. p12.
58 Bordwell, David. Narration in the Fiction Film. Madison, Wisconsin, The University of Wisconsin Press, 1985, P 157.

the classical compositional dominant."[59] According to Bordwell narration in a classical film is mainly motivated 'compositionally'. It may also be motivated 'generically' but less often 'realistically' and very rarely 'artistically'; "The classical technical styles are invisible and transparent in order to not encourage the viewer to examine beneath its smooth surface."[60]

Meir Sternberg characterizes classical narration in three scales: 'self-conscious' (The level of awareness the narration creates for the audience); 'knowledgeable' (How much does the narration know); and 'communicative' (How willing is the narration to tell us what it knows).[61] After the opening part in classical film, the narration's self-consciousness is kept at a minimum and the narration becomes more communicative mainly through the character's actions and reactions. The characters can give the audience information about the story or withhold it if necessary depending on the genre. Although the point of views are not always restricted to 'objective' point of views, but if there are few 'subjective' point of view shots (even the flashbacks) present, the classical film will ensure that these are anchored in an 'objective' frame of reference. Music can be used both as a device to reinforce objective point of view and establish time and place as does an inter-title or a sign. Music also reinforces subjective point of view by expressing characters' mental states.[62] The spatial

59   Bordwell, David. Staiger, Janet and Thompson, Kristin. "Classical narration". The Classical Hollywood Cinema : Film Style and Mode of Production to 1960. Routledge & Kegan Paul, London, Melbourne and Henley, 1985, p21.

60   Ibid. p25.

61   Sternberg, Meir. Expositional Modes and Temporal ordering in Fiction. John Hopkins, University press, 1978, pp 56-57.

62   Bordwell, David. Staiger, Janet and Thompson, Kristin. "Classical narration". The Classical Hollywood Cinema : Film

omnipresence, repetition of story information, minimal changes in temporal order, and plays between restricted and relatively unrestricted points of view, achieve the celebrated Hollywood narration 'continuity'. Musical accompaniment from the start is one of the most overt continuity factor in classical narration.

Based on the differences between classical narration and the Short Cut's narration, it will be appropriate to present a more detailed observation of Short Cut's beginning and the end, hoping this will help to gain a more accurate sense of the film's structure and also the role of audience.

Style and Mode of Production to 1960. Routledge & Kegan Paul, London, Melbourne and Henley, 1985,. p32.

Short Cuts: The Beginning, The End, and The role of Audience

In classical Hollywood cinema the role of spectator is described as inactive or passive. "Because we see no dramatic gaps in narrative continuity, "we never question its source".[63] The first unambiguous and significant information provided in the beginning of the film about the character or situation becomes the basis for audience's expectations for the entire film. This first information acts as a fixed baseline against which later information can be judged by the audience. The Star system has a very significant role in the first impression. Upon for example, the moment we see Julia Roberts we place her in a stereotyped role as we expect romance and entertainment from her. Once the first impression, as called by Meir Sternberg "Primacy effect", is in place, it is very difficult for the spectator to accept something else even if the narrative provides the contrary.[64] This technique reinforced by the star system, is a common way of presenting character change and character development in the classical Hollywood cinema.

---

63 Ibid. p33.
64 Sternberg, Meir. Expositional Modes and Temporal ordering in Fiction. John Hopkins, University press, 1978, pp 56-57.

Short Cuts: The Beginning

A black screen, the sound of helicopters, a view of city lights, helicopter sound continues, music starts, letters are moving over the screen: 'spelling film international presents', music is more audible. The camera pans right to reveal a sign illuminated by the helicopter lights: 'REMEMBER MEDFLY QUARANTINE, no home grown fruits or vegetables to leave area', music takes over. Looking up, helicopters spraying simultaneously insecticide, as more names dance over the screen, 'A Robert Altman Film' (00:00:52), SHORT CUTS (00:00:53). The camera pans off from the helicopters to a white stretch limousine that is cruising along the road. Helicopters fly over the city in formation and spraying, the name of the actors dancing over the screen in no particular order. We hear the voice of a news reader, shortly after we see a TV in the back of the white limousine. An editorial by 'Howard Finnigan' played by Bruce Davison, reports the war on the Medfly (00:02:08): "Time is come to go to war again, not with Iraq, not international terrorists, or what was once Yugoslavia, but with medflies". Camera moves to the limo driver, 'Earl Piggot' played by Tom Waits. Earl turns and looks into the back seat at a man in a tuxedo with a stethoscope around his neck and snuggled with a blonde woman. Earl takes a drink from his hip flask. Howard Finnigan's editorial is running, 'a potentially devastating insect, what... California makes its new home, despite the spraying .... How significant is for the health of public. Cross over to the helicopters spraying the names of the rest of the crew over the screen, we hear Howard Finnigan's voice; public is not convinced. The camera tilts from the dark sky to the Finnigan's house. We view the bed room through first floor window. we see Howard Finnigan sitting on a bed watching his own show. He calls his wife to come and join him and we meet 'Ann Finnigan' played by Andie MacDowell. We see on TV the Finnigan's editorial, "people sense that ...is that a war one can be won? I would say no...How is this war.... The camera is back to the L.A. Skyline. As the helicopters fly in formation over the city, more names dance over the screen. The camera crosses over to 'Zoe Trainer' played by Lori Singer. Zoe plays cello with a quintet in a concert hall. The camera turns to Zoe's audience and we meet 'Clair and Stuart Kane' played by Anne Archer & Red Ward, seated next to 'Marian and Dr. Ralph Wyman' played by Julianne Moore & Matthew Modine. Cross cut to the front of the Kaiser's house, we hear the helicopters and we see 'Jerry Kaiser' played by Chris Penn covering up his truck with a trap. Jerry enters the house and we meet his wife 'Lois' played by Jennifer Jason Leigh. Lois talks sex on the phone while her children are present. In Kaiser's house Howard Finnigan's editorial continues and in the background we hear the helicopters. The helicopters continue lying over the city and more names continue to dance on the screen. The camera pans down and shows a 24-Hour diner. We hear a female voice singing the song 'Prisoner of Life'. We see Earl Piggot's limo pull into a parking spot outside the 24-Hour diner. Earl enters the diner and we meet his wife, waitress 'Doreen Piggot' played by Lily Tomlin. The song continues and the view pans back to the L.A. Skyline and to the helicopters. The camera tilts from the helicopters to a jazz club, where we meet 'Tess Trainer' played by Annie Ross. Tess sings 'Prisoner of Life'. Camera turns towards Tess's audience and we meet 'Bill and Honey Bush' played by Robert Downey JR. & Lili Taylor, sitting at a table with their neighbours. The camera goes back to the sky and helicopters and some more names dance on the screen. We hear Howard Finnigan's editorial talking about water shortage, while we enter the Shepard's living room where the TV is running, and the dog, Suzy is barking outside. We meet 'Sherri Shepard' played by Madeleine Stowe and her three children. The helicopters approach so Sherri runs out to bring Suzy in, and an argument starts between Sherri and her husband 'Gene Shepard' played by Tim Robbins about the danger of insecticides. This conversation upsets Gene and he leaves the house enraged. Camera back to the skyline and helicopters but this time 'Directed by Robert Altman', dances from top left to down right (00:09:08). At this point the camera crosses from the concert hall to the Kaiser's house, to a jazz club, to the Finnigan house, where we meet the Finnigan's boy 'Casey' played by Zane Cassidy. This is when Howard's editorial ends: "This is Howard Finnigan with thoughts to make you think.". We hear Zoe's cello playing and the camera goes back to the skyline. The colour of the sky indicates the sun rise and the helicopters land. We meet 'William "Stormy" Weather' played by Peter Gallagher who is one of the helicopter pilots. Stormy goes to a telephone booth to call his ex-wife and wish her a happy birthday. Intercut with the next scene we see Betty Weather's house. The phone rings and we meet Betty's young son, 'Chad' played by Jarret Lennon and 'Betty' played by Frances McDormand who hangs up on Stormy. The Camera crosses to the Kane's where Claire Kane puts on white makeup and we see an array of clown paraphernalia in her dressing room. Claire's husband Stuart is packing his backpack and after a short conversation with Claire he leaves with his two friends for a fishing trip without saying goodbye to Claire. The camera goes back to Betty Weather's house and we discover that Gene Shepard is having an affair with Betty.

The Camera crosses to Finnigan's pool area, where Jerry Kaiser comes to clean the pool. We see that Zoe Trainer lives next door. After a short visit to see Bill & Honey Bush we are back to Finnigan's pool area. Ann Finnigan is concerned about the effect of insecticides on the pool water as it is Casey's birthday on Saturday. Casey wants to swim but he has allergies, Jerry Kaiser ensures her that the water is safe. We see Zoe's mother, the jazz singer Tess Trainer, standing on the next door house balcony (00:18:19).

Short Cuts starts at a very fast pace. There are thirty one sequences (two every one minutes on average) in the first 18 minutes. The viewers are bombarded with information. The continuity is maintained by sound (the sound of helicopters), the music (Tess Trainer's song) and similarity between the objects. For example one door closes in one household at the end of a sequence another door opens in a different household in the beginning of the next sequence. There are also other devices to help the continuity such as the appearance of television continuing showing Howard Filligan's editorial as the camera moves from one household to the other. Within minutes into the film we are aware of time and location, we are warned about some natural disasters, and in the following ten to fifteen minutes we are introduced to nine couples and families. We know how their houses look like, we know their occupation, how many children they have and the nature of their relationships. We know that Earl Piggot has a drinking problem and that this causes problems between him and his wife Doreen. We are informed that Shepards argue a lot and that Gene Shepard, who is trying to give up smoking, is having an affair with Betty Weather. Stormy Weather is still not over the separation from Betty and is angry. Kane's are not as happy as they used to be. We know that Lois Kaiser works as a telephone sex sales woman and her husband Jerry Kaiser is very unhappy about her occupational choice. Ralph Wyman acts very irritable towards his wife Marian. We sense that Tess Trainer might be depressed, and might have a drinking problem, and that Zoe Trainer is obsessed with her Cello. We know about the relationship between the Finnigan family and that they are preparing for their son's birthday. We know how the couple Honey and Bill Bush are like and their relationship to their neighbours.

Bordwell describes the beginning of classical narrative as more self-conscious and omnipresent than communicative: "Classical narration usually begins before the action does."[65] He points out the importance of the the title and the roles of the stars in the beginning of a classical narration sequence: "The title will most probably describe the main character or the main action, or the time of the action", and the stars: "credits listing the cast may reinforce the title or introduce the film's narrative hierarchy."[66] The title Short Cuts neither indicates the nature, nor the location or the time of the action. In an interview to David Breskin in 1991 Altman titled the film 'L.A. Short Cuts'.[67] This was most likely Altman's choice to lure the studios into financing the production. Short Cuts, has an ensemble cast with twenty two principle actors. The lack of hierarchy in presenting the names of the cast, is in contrary of the rules of classical Hollywood cinema. Altman's ensemble cast challenges the role of the

65 Bordwell, David, Staiger, Janet, Thompson, Kristin. The Classical Hollywood Cinema: Film style & mode of production to 1960. Routledge & Kegan Paul, London, Melbourne and Henley, 1985, p 25.
66 Ibid.
67 Breskin, David. Inner Views: Filmmaker in conversation. Faber and Faber, Boston, London, 1992, p 317.

stars within the classical Hollywood narration , for their creating the first impression and character development.

Bordwell's formalist approach describes the narrative film as consisting of three systems: narrative logic, the representation of time, and representation of space. Bordwell believes that there is a marked hierarchy of systems in classical film and one system will always dominate the others. "In Hollywood cinema 'a specific sort of narrative causality operates as the dominant' making temporal and spatial systems vehicles for it."[68] Bordwell chooses the terms used by the Russian formalist literary critics, who distinguished between Fabula (story) and Syuzhet (plot). Bordwell describes the 'plot' as the actual film before us, including all the three systems manifested in the film as described above. The 'story' is the viewer's subjective mental construct, "a structure of inferences we make on the basis of selected aspects of the plot."[69]

In Short Cuts, time and space appear disrupted or fractured, making a presentation of a straightforward Hollywood 'plot' difficult to situate. But in a way Short Cuts seems to have "one story" or "one look" that Altman likes to give to the audience: an Altmanian look of Raymond Carver's stories and the poem Lemonade."[70] By bringing the all nine stories together in the first twenty minutes of Short Cuts, Altman masterfully achieves his goal to give 'one look' to all nine Raymond Carver stories. Connecting the stories through the characters' entering in

---

68   Bordwell, David, Staiger, Janet, Thompson, Kristin. The Classical Hollywood Cinema: Film style & mode of production to 1960. Routledge & Kegan Paul, London, Melbourne and Henley, 1985, p 12.

69   Ibid.

70   Carver, Raymond. Short Cuts, "with an Introduction by Robert Altman", The Harvill Press, London, 1993, p 7.

each others space, is also an intelligent device to help the audience to connect and remember.

Short Cuts: The End

John Belton describes how classical narrative routinely begins with an act that disturbs the original state of things but all is resolved at the end of the film. Some similar disturbances continue to happen in the classical narrative all through the film, "helping the narrative to move towards closure, completion, and conclusion."[71]

Altman describes Short Cuts as only an observation of "idiosyncrasies of human behaviour". "It is more about what you don't know than what you do know." The film could 'go on forever' because it is like life, "Lifting the roof off the Weathers' home and seeing Stormy decimate his furniture with a skill saw, then lifting off another roof, the Kaisers', or the Waymans', or the Shepherds', and seeing some different behaviour."[72] Nothing is 'resolved' at the end of Short Cuts and it doesn't end with any closure, completion or conclusion as such. As Altman describes, it is like life and it 'can go for ever'. Therefore a focus on the last twenty minutes of Short Cuts, might give us a better understanding of Altman's idea of endings.

We see Marian Wayman and Claire Kane descend the spiral staircase at Waymans' house dressed in clown suits and singing. Stuart asks Ralph about dead bodies. Claire suggests a little make up and costume for Ralph and Stuart, stating, 'weird behaviour', isn't that what it's all about? Ralph wants to be 'nothing' and Claire suggests

---

71 Belton, John. American Cinema/American Culture. Rutgers University, McGraw-Hill, New York, 1994, pp 22-23.
72 Carver, Raymond. Short Cuts, "with an Introduction by Robert Altman", The Harvill Press, London, 1993, p 7.

erasing his face. Claire sings a song while putting make up on Ralph's face. It is a song about a girl drowning in a river as she cries for help. Stuart responds angrily, 'but he couldn't help her, she was dead'. We see the Finnigans' house, where Ann wakes up with a sudden revelation. She tells Howard that she knows it was the baker, Mr. Bitkower, who made the disturbing telephone calls. We see Tess in the Jazz club, she sings "I Don't Know You". At Waymans' patio, it is sunrise. Ralph now wears a clown face and blows up balloons and Stuart sketches Marion. He tells her that her mother was an artist and she tells him about her teacher at art school who killed himself. At the Trainers' house, Tess pulls into the driveway, gets out of her car, hears an engine, sees exhaust seeping out, opens the garage door and discovers Zoe's dead body. At the Bakery, Ann Finnigan confronts Mr. Bitkower angrily about his telephone calls and informs him that Casey is dead. 'My son is dead. He is dead, Mr. Bitkower. He was hit by a car the day I ordered the cake. We've been waiting with him in the hospital until he died. There are no more birthdays, you bastard'. Ann starts hitting him. Mr. Bitkower is shocked. He brings two chairs and asks the couple to sit down. Over to a one-hour photo shop, where the Kaisers and the Bushes arrive to pick up their pictures, and by accident see the pictures of a girl's dead body in a river taken by Gordon Johnson. At Piggots' trailer, Doreen and Earl have Hawaiian leis around their necks while they drink and enjoy each other's company. We see Betty very happy in a red Mustang convertible driven by her lover, an airline pilot.We see Kaisers and Bushs arriving in the canyons, where Jerry and Bill meet two Young girls, Barbara and Nancy riding their bicycles. Bill and Jerry follow the girls telling Lois and Honey they are going for a smoke. At the bakery, Mr. Bitkower carries a tray of muffins to the Finnigans. Betty arrives home but when she opens the door she is too shocked to speak. There are pieces of damaged furniture all around, the carpet clean and the TV is running. Back to the canyon Barbara and Nancy stop with their bikes, Bill and Jerry approach them and offer them some beer, Bill leaves with Barbara to a bat cave, Nancy stays with Jerry, while cleaning her shirt, Jerry picks up a rock and starts clubbing Nancy. Suddenly there is a rumble, a group of birds flying off in all directions, and the sound of falling rocks. It is an earthquake. Jerry's face is spattered with blood. Nancy is dead on the ground. We see Lois, Honey and Kaiser's kids to experience the earthquake and at the Bakery, Finnigans and Mr. Bitkower are hiding under the table, as baking sheets fall all around them. At Shepards' house, Sherri gathers her kids and Gene stands on the patio with a bullhorn, screaming 'This is Officer Gene Shepard of the LAPD, We are currently experiencing an earthquake'. At the Trainer house, Tess is drunk and singing. She seems to be unaware of the earthquake. In the Waymans' house, Marian, Ralph, Claire and Stuart are in the Jacuzzi, and Stuart says 'Don't worry! It's not a big one'. Betty is in her house and still in shock and Chad pulls her arm to move her out of house. The Piggots do not appear to be disturbed by the earthquake. Still in good mood, kissing and laughing. Gene Shepard continues to direct neighbours with his bullhorn. After the earthquake stops he goes over to his family to put his arms around Sherri and the kids and pulls them close to him. In the Waymans' house the Waymans and Kanes climb out of the Jacuzzi, get into the house to eat and watch TV. They hear that fifteen people were injured and a young woman was killed by falling rocks. Stuart repeats that one person was killed, and Claire claims that one fatality is not really so bad. Stormy Weather is interviewed on TV. The Wymans and the Kanes walk back to the patio and drink tequila together as they toast to "lemonade". As the camera pans away from them, the music increases. Tess sings "Prisoner of Life" and camera continues to move across the patio and slowly to sweeping view of Los Angeles county.

Altman's masterful use of natural disaster in the beginning and the end of Short Cuts, not only represents the reality of life in California, but also makes the film coherent, and not only by connecting the characters in the film, but also by connecting the film with the audience and the rest of the world.

Altman said that he doesn't like to create "satisfactory" endings, as he doesn't believe anything in life stops. "The only ending I know about is death." Altman describes that the endings in some of his films like The Player or M*A*S*H are rather manipulated endings: "Those aren't endings, they are stopping places."[73] It seems if the ending in Short Cuts is more than a 'satisfactory' ending as it ends with death: one accidental death, two murders and one suicide, or with talks about death.

Short Cuts: The role of Audience

In A Cinema of Loneliness, Robert Kolker describes how Altman's attempt to dissociate himself from the rigid forms of classical Hollywood storytelling and to create the appearance of spontaneity and improvisation in an arbitrary and calculated way, helps to place the viewer in the narrative in a specific way.[74]

73 Breskin, David. Inner Views: Filmmaker in conversation. Faber and Faber, Boston, London, 1992, pp 301-302.
74 Kolker, Robert Philip. A Cinema of Loneliness. Third Edition, Oxford University Press, New York, 2000, pp 332-333.

Altman said he hopes with his films to "train the audience" and bring them along with him; "If they come there and sit in front of their sets or in the theatre, and they don't go halfway with you, and don't take the material in front of them and process it through their own history, it's meaningless. If they do even they might not have any idea what that was about, but feel that it was right and they know that it fits."[75] Altman believed that the audience need always to try something new even if they are unable to express this wish or even not able to recognised if something new is offered to them. Altman seems to project his own need for novelty and new challenges, onto the audience: "When I see that everything is very safe, I think it isn't any fun for me,…, unless it's a real stretch, a real uphill climb, unless I'm doing some thing that I don't think can be done."[76]

Short Cuts with its fast pace and with nine stories starting simultaneously, is a big challenge for the audience to follow. Short Cuts not only needs viewers' full concentration and intellectual involvement, but also needs the awareness of audiences' emotional and psychological states. Robert T. Self describes Short Cuts as a perfect example of Altman forcing the viewer to import their patterns of personality, relationships, and motivation to the movie.[77] Altman expects the audience to take the challenge intellectually as well as to increase their imagination and their ability to hold on of one character even when the camera is focusing on the other characters. Altman is

75 Ibid.
76 Breskin, David. Inner Views: Filmmaker in conversation. Faber and Faber, Boston, London, 1992, p 290.
77 Self, Robert. T. Robert Altman's Subliminal Reality. University of Minnesota Press, Minneapolis, London, 2002, p247.

fascinated by the idea that millions of people who might have watched Short Cuts, might have different thoughts and images about what happened to the characters during these 'gaps'. That is what Altman hoped to achieve with his films and that is what he thought that it does make a movie interesting. [78] In contrast to traditional classical cinema Altman's ambition was to develop his art, to connect to his environment rather than to ensure a box office success.

Altman compares his expectations of his audience to Raymond Carver's expectations of his readers. Altman describes how Carver's stories are about what one doesn't know rather than what one does know and that "the reader fills in the gaps, while recognizing the undercurrents." [79] Both Classical Hollywood Cinema and Altman, use the term "filling in the gaps" as an expected role of the audience. Although 'gap filling' in traditional Hollywood cinema is fully calculated and controlled in order to entertain and give the audience the illusion of participation to secure the box office profit, in Altman's cinema and particularly in Short Cuts, the term is meant to work towards the fast pace of the film and cross cut stories. Bordwell describes how classical narration may force the spectator to shape hypotheses by creating some permanent or temporary gaps and holding back the information. But in contrast he believes that the common practise of Hollywood narration is to ask the spectator to form hypotheses that are highly probable and sharply exclusive. "By threading together several probable and quite exclusive hypotheses, we participate in a game of controlled expectation and

---

78 Breskin, David. Inner Views: Filmmaker in conversation. Faber and Faber, Boston, London, 1992, p 290.
79 Carver, Raymond. Short Cuts, "with an Introduction by Robert Altman", The Harvill Press, London, 1993, p 7.

likely confirmation."[80] These gaps in classical narration are continually and systematically opened and filled in, no gap is permanent, narration remains fundamentally reliable and we are not led to any invalid conclusions or unpredictable endings, but mainly to some kind of happy endings. The spectator is conditioned to expect how a good story should unfold, in order to be entertained. Bordwell believes that this places Hollywood as the dominant force with a total control.

Christian Metz points out that traditional film presents itself to the audience, as history and not as discourse. He argues that transparent film, with a narrative that appears to tell almost everything, is based on a denial that anything is absent or that anything has to be discovered. Hence it is like a history, which is always about 'completed' events. Metz further argues that we see only the "reverse and always more or less regressive face of those factors", the one which are completed and satisfied, "the formulated accomplishment of an unformulated wish."[81] Metz describes his relationship to the film as both passive, semi active and active: as "witness and helper", "I watch, and I aid". He compares this role to the role of a midwife who attends at a birth; "in watching the film I help it to be born, I help it to live, since it is in me that it will live and it was made for that, to be seen, i.e. to come into existence only when it is seen."[82]

Altman also in favour of changing the role of audience

---

80 Bordwell, David. Staiger, Janet and Thompson, Kristin. "Classical narration". The Classical Hollywood Cinema : Film Style and Mode of Production to 1960. Routledge & Kegan Paul, London, Melbourne and Henley, 1985, p38.

81 Metz, Christian. "History/discourse: a note on two voyeurisms". In John Caughie (Ed.) Theories of Authorship: A Reader. Ruthledge, London and New York, 2001, p226.

82 Ibid. p 227.

and their expectations of themselves , does not express this in the same way as Metz. Altman wants to touch the audience on an "unconscious basis to where they sense something rather than intellectually know or agree to something." [83] Altman wants very much the audience to make an investment in his films and to see them "emotionally, rather than intellectually." [84]

Altman's idea of a great movie is a very nonlinear one, something that the audience will watch where they will walk away not able to articulate what they think about it. Altman doesn't feel that he has something to preach or something to say: "It's just painting what I see...To show people something beyond the scope of where they are standing is a fantastic thing."[85] Unlike Hollywood cinema, Altman likes to convince the audience of preference of his perception of art cinema. Hence it is time now to explore more the development of American cinema after 1960s as well as the role of Robert Altman in this development.

83 Altman, Robert. Scene commentary. The Player. 1992. Videodisc. Santa Monica, Calif.: Voyager, 1992.
84 Kass, M. Judith. Robert Altman: American Innovator. Popular Library, a Unit of CBS Publication, USA, 1978, p 9.
85 Ibid.

The 'Post' Classical Hollywood Cinema

"A Film is – or should be- more like music than like fiction. It should be a progression of moods and feelings. The theme, what's behind the emotion, the meaning, all that comes later." (Stanley Kubrick)[86]

"The New Hollywood"; "American Art Cinema"; Hollywood's "New Wave"; "movie brats" are all terms which are used to describe the movement in the Hollywood cinema since 1960s. The 'New Wave' filmmaker like Jewson, Penn and Kuberic approached Hollywood cinema from their background in television. Their films were praised for their location shooting, improvisational acting, and experimentation with camera, colour and sound, all devices borrowed from the European New Wave. Also the so called 'movie brats' like Spielberg, de Palma, Lucas, Coppola, and Scorsese came to Hollywood with a sophisticated understanding of the new film techniques.

Steve Neale describes three major variations between the old and the new Hollywood cinema in terms of changes in mise-en-scene, characters, and conventions of presenting subject matter. He explains that "dramatic and spatio-temporal unity founded in classical mise-en-

86 www.raindance.co.uk/newsletter

scene gives way to overtly articulated mise-en-scene as zoom and telephoto lenses, slow-motion, and split-screen devices". Characters also change from a "goal-oriented hero" to troubled, introspective protagonists. Due to changes in mise-en-scene and characters, narrative fragmentation replaces the linear plot and narrative, which subsequently alters the conventions of presenting subject matter. "Genres fall apart" but they are "replaced by a realism compromised by traditional dramatic values."[87] Neale argues that despite the changes in narration, the effect on the spectator remains the same, and if there are some difficulties for the spectators, there might be sought in difficulties of the communication referred to a human source, for example to the director as "auteur", as a possible way for "spectators to use authorship to make the experience coherent."[88]

Bordwell and Thompson describe that by the mid 1960s cinema was already established as a vital contemporary art due to the achievements of post-war European modernism, the increasing influence of the auteur idea, and new developments in documentary and experimental film.[89] They believe that the birth of the New Hollywood cinema was a rather logical consequence of the late 1960s recession in American film industry, as was the fact that older directors retired, and the 'movie brats' took their place. Robert Altman and Woody Allen are labeled as the first generation of movie brats. Bordwell and Thompson argue that the need to search for new audiences forced Hollywood to open its door to new filmmakers who

---

87   Neale, Steve. "New Hollywood Cinema". Screen 17, no.2, Summer 1976, pp 117-122.
88   Ibid.
89   Bordwell, David and Thompson, Kristin. Film History: An Introduction. McGraw-Hill, New York, 2003, p 506.

wanted to create art films. These new filmmaker adapted storytelling techniques pioneered in the European art cinema by emphasising on mood, characterisation, and psychological ambiguity.[90] For example Stanley Kubric's 2001: A space Odyssey (1968) was compared to Federico Fellini's films or Michaelangelo Antonioni during the 1960s. Bordwell suggests that although the contemporary Hollywood cinema in 1960s absorbed narrational strategies of the art cinema, it remained stable by controlling these new narrational strategies within a coherent genre framework.[91]

The term 'post-classical' was suggested first in 1990s by Henry Jenkins in his essay "Historical Poetics" and describes both continuities and breaks with classical cinema.[92] In his essay Historical Poetics, Henry Jenkins points out that Bordwells' argument fails to acknowledge the necessary process of experimentation and accommodation which is associated with the adoption of new and unfamiliar aesthetic norms into the dominant classical system.[93] Jenkins suggests that the each new generation of American filmmakers since mid 1960s brought "new formal elements" into classical Hollywood cinema, which further broadened the system and increased its own market potential and satisfied a "media-savvy

90   Ibid.
91   Bordwell, David. Staiger, Janet and Thompson, Kristin. "Classical narration". The Classical Hollywood Cinema : Film Style and Mode of Production to 1960. Routledge & Kegan Paul, London, Melbourne and Henley, 1985, p 377.
92   Jenkins,.Henry. "Historical Poetics". In Hollows, Hutchings and Jancovich (Eds.), Manchester ; New York: Manchester University Press, 1995, p 113.
93   Jenkins,.Henry. "Historical Poetics". In Hollows, Hutchings and Jancovich (Eds.), p 114.

audience" for novelty and innovation.[94] Jenkins agrees with Bordwell that in this whole process, film aesthetics were more under influence rather than the narrative's depth or complexity. Jenkins continues that over time, accommodating of these stylistic experiments in the system made them 'invisible' and the films remained fully comprehensible according to traditional classical criteria of causality, coherence and continuity.[95]

Bordwell and Thompson believe that "many of the New Hollywood directors self-consciously returned to the traditions of the classical studio genres".[96] Altman was certainly not one of these many filmmakers and his films continued to follow the principle of the art cinema and to resist the mainstream Hollywood cinema by radiating a "distrust of authority, a criticism of American pieties, and a celebration of energetic, if confused, idealism."[97] In 1975 Robin Wood listed the central contribution of Altman's work to the development of the modern American cinema, in his growing sense of disorientation and confusion of values with a consequent sapping of any possibilities for affirmation, in his critical attitude towards the Hollywood's traditional genres with his awareness of the modern European cinema and his desire to assimilate its techniques, and also in his attempt to change the role and status of the director from studio employee to all determining artist.[98]

---

94 Ibid. p 115.
95 Ibid. p 116.
96 Ibid. p516-517.
97 Bordwell, David and Thompson, Kristin. Film History: An Introduction. McGraw-Hill, New York, 2003, p 520.
98 Wood, Robin. "Smart-Ass Cutie-Pie: Notes toward an Evaluation of Robert Altman."Movie, No. 21, Autumn 1975, p 1-17.

Robert Altman's Life and Cinema

Robert Bernard Altman was born in 1925 in Kansas City, Missouri, USA. He was the first son of Bernard (B.C) Altman, a charismatic and successful insurance salesman and Helen Mathews, in contrast to B.C., more sensible and low-key. B.C. is described as carefree with money and a gambler. Robert Altman is the first grand son in the Altman dynasty. The Altman family was part of the early foundation of modern Kansas City. The family name was originally spelled as in German 'Altmann' with two n's. Altman's great-grandfather, Clement Altman was a respectable linen manufacturer in Germany, before he migrated to America in the late 1840s. Clement married Altman's great-grandmother in 1852 or 1853, also from a German catholic background and they settled in Kansas City. Their fourth eldest son, Frank Sr., Altman's grandfather, was a entrepreneur, who opened his second jewelry store in Kansas City in 1882, at the age of twenty one. Frank Sr. did so well financially that he extended his business into the real estate industry, an area with an unlimited gain. He erected several important buildings in Kansas City, including the 'American Hotel Building', the seven-story fire proof 'New Centre Building', and the head quarters for the 'Calvin Company', where Robert

Altman first started his career in the film industry. Altman's maternal grand mother Nettie Bolt was also from a German background. Nettie was a talented concert pianist and one of the generations of Germans obsessed with culture. Nettie passed down her appreciation and love for music and the classical arts particularly to her daughters. Nettie's three daughters studied music both in the USA and in Europe. They became harpists, pianists, and singers. As the eldest of three in the company of his younger sisters, Altman was fortunate to grew up in the company of his talented and artistic aunts. In an interview Altman mentions the impact of growing up with these creative women, as discernible in his art.[99] Altman attended St.Peters Catholic School and Rockhurst High School before he was sent to Wentworth Military Academy in Lexington, Missouri in the middle of his junior years. He enlisted in the Air Force and became a co-pilot of a B-24 when he was just nineteen years old. After the end of World War II, he started his career making industrial films for the Calvin Company in Kansas City. [100]

Altman worked at Calvin Company as a writer, photographer, producer, set designer, director, and film editor until he was noticed by Alfred Hitchcock and was hired to direct some episodes of the TV series Alfred Hitchcock Presents. He was employed by the television till the mid sixties, and directed several TV series including some episodes of Bonanza in 1959. Altman's work was considered by industry bosses to be controversial mostly because of his strong tendency for having more than one

99 Berskin, David. Inner views: Filmmaker in conversation. Faber and Faber, Boston, London, 1992, pp 284-285..

100 McGilligan, Patrick. Jumping off the Cliff: A Biography of The Great American Director. St. Martin's Press, New York, 1989, pp 3-45.

voice on the sound track at the same time and for his habit of rewriting scripts. Finally he quit television altogether as he didn't want to become "one of those hundreds of creative people who have just died on television."[101] After a period of unemployment, Altman found a way to break into the feature films when he was hired by Warner Brothers to direct Countdown in 1968, a science fiction film about the American-Soviet space race. His next project That Cold Day in the Park (1969) represents Altman's tendency to experiment with his overlapping sound techniques and innovative camera movements. This technique is described by Robert Kolker, in A Cinema of Loneliness, as 'decentralisation' of space, both visual and aural. Altman was the first director to introduce the multi-layered sound tracks into films which at the time were ground breaking in motion picture sound technology.

1970 was Altman's break through with M*A*S*H, a project which was offered to him after it was rejected by more than a dozen other directors. Altman liked the black humour in the plot and could use his experience with war-related material during his working on several episodes of 'Combat'. M*A*S*H was a massive box-office success and Altman collected the Cannes Palme d'or and five Oscar nominations including one for the best director. After his success with M*A*S*H, the following five or six films made by Altman were not box-office hits. The 1970s was also a difficult time for Altman as regard his relationship with the big studios, which were experiencing financial crisis and had little interest in a demanding director who wanted to have artistic freedom, to employ his distinctive style and an original approach that opposed conventional Hollywood storytelling. Despite this Altman's career

101 Kass, M. Judith. Robert Altman: American Innovator. Popular Library, a Unit of CBS Publication, USA, 1978, p 9.

in the 1970s was regarded as one of his most fruitful periods specifically with one of his most ambitious films Nashville (1975). Altman was dropped by the big studios altogether in the beginning of the 1980s after his Paramount production Popeye (1980) turned out to be a box-office disappointment. During the 1980s he produced and directed a series of low-budget adaptations of stage plays, but the audience appeal was very limited. In 1990 Altman stopped directing plays, after Vincent and Theo, a French-British co-production brought him back into the public eye. But Altman's major comeback was his success with The Player (1992), a film regarded by many as Altman's revenge on Hollywood. A Rolling Stone interview describes Altman's return as following:

"Just when we thought we wouldn't have Altman to kick around any more, he came back with three impressive pieces: Tanner '88, in which he and Garry Trudeau ran a fictional character for president, was a clever and compelling mix of fact and fiction made for HBO. Vincent and Theo, in 1990, emerged as a slashing portrayal of a punkish Van Gogh and his brother and resurrected Altman's high-art credentials. And now, improbably back to Hollywood waltzes this aging, acid dumpling of a man, where he turns out a killer – The Player- masquerading as a sheepish fluffy comedy."[102]

His subsequent film Short Cuts in 1993, was compared to Nashville and won the Golden Lion Best Film Award at the 1993 Venice Film Festival. Altman's films are consistently described as challenging, innovative, enigmatic, and idiosyncratic. Robert Altman was criticised for his desire to be "different" with his films having

---

102 Berskin, David. "I Try to Debunk Myself as Much as Anybody Else': Interview with Robert Altman." Rolling Stone, 16 April 1992, pp 74-77, 86, 94-95.

wandering storylines, incomprehensible characters, and a lack of pace. He was described as careless and unimaginative for the use of the slow zoom and for his preference for shooting only a few takes of a scene and was criticised by some actors, who were used to being given more time by the directors to develop their characters.[103] Bordwell and Thompson describe Altman as the 'only' director who persistently made efforts to maintain a Hollywood 'art cinema' after the mid-1970s. They describe Altman's style as idiosyncratic, with a restless pan-and-zoom camera style, abrupt cutting, multiple shooting which keeps the viewpoint outside the character action and with semi-improvised performances, where characters mumble, interrupt each other and talk simultaneously.[104]

In his book, Robert Altman's Subliminal Reality, Robert T. Self examines in detail twenty-one of Altman's films from 1968 to 2000. T. Self claims that all Altman's films present a clear relationship between the story form of the art film, the social subject of contemporary culture, and the system of popular culture entertainment. To T. Self these films "both adhere to and embody the characteristics of art-cinema narration", rather than being the work of a cinematic auteur of personal movies.[105] T. Self believes that the "subliminal reality" in Altman's films display the continuing vitality of an American art cinema:

"Altman's concept of subliminal reality assumes that communication exists on many levels simultaneously.

103 O'Brien, Daniel. Robert Altman, Hollywood Survivor. B.T. Batsford Ltd, London, 1995, p 13.
104 Bordwell, David and Thompson, Kristin. Film History: An Introduction. McGraw-Hill, New York, 2003, p 520.
105 Self, T. Robert. Robert Altman's Subliminal Reality. University of Minnesota Press, Minneapolis, London, 2002, Introduction ix.

It assumes human interaction motivated by chance, ambiguity, and uncertainty. It recognizes that whatever stories or people seem to say on the surface in sequential, grammatically and temporally linear fashion, a subsurface meaning emerges from metaphoric and symbolic associations.[…] Altman motivates modes of storytelling at odds with traditional Hollywood narratives and demands similarly divergent strategies of reading….Altman's films require attention to loose or broken narrative coherence, to multiple and illusive characterisation, and to self-conscious reflections on systems of entertainment.[…] The audience must simultaneously engage models of narrative organisation, social psychology, and modernist reflexivity in order to follow the logic of these strands of significance. […] Subliminal reality at once denotes a method of narration in Robert Altman films and the complex of demands that art-cinema method places upon spectators who view the films for pleasure and understanding…".[106]

Robert Altman is described as one of the most genuinely innovative, idiosyncratic, influential and independent American filmmakers. Since his first feature film, The Delinquents in 1957, a low-budget teenage angst drama, he directed more than forty feature films and several TV series. After Short Cuts Altman directed Pret-a-Porter (Ready to Wear) in 1994, Kansas City in 1996, Gingerbread Man in 1998, Cookie's Fortune in 1999, Dr. T & The Women in 2000, Gosford Park in 2001, The Company in 2003 and A Prairie Home Companion in 2006. Altman was still developing new projects until his death, including a film based on 1997's Hands on a Hard Body: The Documentary. Altman was nominated for Oscars five times for Best Director but never won. In February 2006 the Academy of Motion Picture Arts and

106 Ibid. pp3-7.

Sciences awarded Altman an Academy Honorary Award for Lifetime Achievement. During his acceptance speech, Altman revealed that he had received a heart transplant approximately ten or eleven years earlier. Altman then said perhaps the Academy had acted prematurely in recognizing the body of his work, as he felt like he might have four more decades of life ahead of him.

Sadly on 20 November 2006, Altman died at the age 81 at Cedars-Sinai Medical Center in Los Angeles reportedly as a consequence of leukemia. Paul Thomas Anderson dedicated his film There Will Be Blood (2007) to Robert Altman. Anderson was Altman's standby director for A Prairie Home Companion in the event that Altman was unable to finish shooting. In 2009 the University of Michigan won the bid to archive approximately 900 boxes of his personal papers, scripts, legal, business and financial records, photographs, props and related material. The total collection measures over 1,000 linear feet. Altman filmed Secret Honor as well as directed several operas at the school. [107]

---

107 Wikipedia, July 2011.

Conclusion

Short Cuts is a unique movie by a unique American filmmaker. Robert Altman once said in an interview in 2004 that Short Cuts is one of the best movies he ever made and I totally agree with him. Short Cuts is about inside and not outside, Short Cuts is like life and can go for ever,...and that is why after almost twenty years we still connect with the film and can not get that out of our minds. Twenty years after Short Cuts was shot, the United States and the world continue to deal with wars, international terrorism, major economic and environmental crises and natural disasters. There continue to be riots and revolts and fear of uncertainties. We can keep watching Short Cuts and identify with the fear and helplessness of those characters and feel comforted by Robert Altman that tells us that they are more things we don't know that we do know and that life will go for ever.

Hasti Sardashti, California, August 2011

About The Author

Hasti Sardashti left Iran in 1984 like so many other young people who left Iran at that time due to the social and political upheaval in the country. She never reached her final destination but happened to arrive in (West) Germany, where she stayed and studied medicine. In 1997 she left Germany to England where she did a masters degree in Film studies and few years later one in the Art therapy maybe on her search to revive her passion for films and arts in general and return to her creative roots. She works part time as a child psychiatrist & psychotherapist and she also paints. She never published a book before.